T0014781

This is a fictionalised biography describing some of the key moments (so far!) in the career of Erling Haaland.
Some of the events described in this book are based upon the author's imagination and are probably not entirely accurate representations of what actually happened.

Tales from the Pitch
Haaland
by Harry Coninx

Published in the United State of American and Canada
by Leapfrog Press
www.leapfrogpress.com

ISBN: 978-1-948585-79-8
First published in 2024

Distributed in the United States by
Consortium Book Sales and Distribution
St Paul, Minnesota, 55114
www.cbsd.com

First published in the United Kingdom (2023 second edition 2024)
by Raven Books
An imprint of Ransom Publishing Ltd.
Unit 7, Brocklands Farm, West Meon, Hampshire GU32 1JN, UK
www.ransom.co.uk

TALES FROM THE PITCH

ERLING HAALAND

HARRY CONINX

Leapfrog Press
New York and London

For Else, the only other Norwegian I know

CONTENTS

I

DREAM DEBUT

January 2020, WWK Arena, Augsburg, Germany
FC Augsburg v Borussia Dortmund

Erling thumped the seat next to him in anger, as Augsburg tucked away their third goal.

He closed his eyes, listening to the chants of the fans. It was all going wrong. This was supposed to be his big day, his first game for Borussia Dortmund. But instead they were being thrashed – and he hadn't even got on the pitch yet.

His new manager, Lucien Favre, turned away from the pitch in disgust and looked up towards the bench.

"Erling!" he shouted. "Start warming up!"

Erling rose from his seat, pulled up his socks and started jogging up and down the touchline. He heard a ripple of applause and a cheer from the Dortmund fans in the far corner. They were desperate for him to get on the pitch, desperate to see their new signing in action.

He stood next to Giovanni Reyna as they both warmed up. Erling felt like a giant next to him.

"You nervous, Erling?"

"No, I'm frustrated. I want to get on and help."

"I think it's just good to get on the pitch, get some minutes under your belt, right?"

Erling shrugged. He didn't see things that way. He hadn't moved to Borussia Dortmund just to make up the numbers, to get some experience. He was determined to make an impact.

He'd only just started his warm-up when Favre called him back over. The manager didn't want to waste any more time before getting his new signing on the pitch.

"We need you out there," Favre said, reaching up

and putting a hand on Erling's shoulder. "We're 3-1 down – let's see what you can do."

Standing on the touchline, Erling took a deep breath. He never felt nervous before a game – he hadn't for a long time – but now he could feel the nerves starting to build.

This was his first game for the club, the first time the Dortmund fans were going to see him in action. He was finally playing in one of the biggest leagues in the world – and he had to prove that he belonged here.

He was desperate to impress.

He bumped fists with Łukasz Piszczek, who was coming off, and seconds later he was on the pitch.

His impact was immediate.

Jadon Sancho moved in from the left-hand side and Erling saw his chance.

"Jadon! Now!" he roared, his voice carrying over the shouts of the fans. It was an inch-perfect ball from Jadon and Erling didn't even need to look at the keeper or the goal. He knew already what he was going to do.

He hit it first-time with his left foot and it flew into the far corner, bouncing in off the post.

GOAL!

Erling didn't stop to savour the cheers of the crowd, or even celebrate in front of his new fans. He raced over to the ball, scooped it out of the goal, then turned and sprinted back towards the half-way line, desperate to get the game back underway.

"Let's win this one now, lads," he shouted.

He didn't even stop to consider what a perfect start this was to his Dortmund career. He'd scored on his debut – and with his very first touch!

But that didn't matter. The important thing was getting the team back in the game and getting the three points.

Two minutes later, Dortmund were back on level terms. A lofted ball from Mats Hummels was expertly controlled by Sancho. Jadon and Erling were both a yard clear of the defenders and they raced in on goal.

"Jadon! Square it!" Erling roared, hungry for another goal. But this time Sancho ignored him, instead choosing to skip around the keeper and tap it into the empty net.

"Next time, you square it to me!" Erling shouted, as they celebrated.

"I set you up for the last one," Jadon laughed, pushing him off.

The Dortmund players and fans were going wild with excitement now, but Erling kept his focus. At 3-3 and with half an hour left, the game was there to be won. He wanted more goals.

Another great ball over the top sent Thorgan Hazard sprinting clear, racing into space. Erling chased after him, keen to get in on the action and get another goal. Hazard rounded the keeper, but the angle was too tight.

"Thorgan! Square it!" Erling roared once more.

This time, his team-mate listened to him and directed the ball into his path. Erling had a clear shot and tapped the ball over the line.

GOAL!

He turned to celebrate, but stopped when he saw Thorgan's face.

"Offside," Thorgan moaned, pointing at the linesman. "I'm sure I timed my run, though. I'm sure I was on."

There were a tense few moments in the stadium as the referee put his finger to his ear, listening to the

VAR. Both sets of fans were quiet, not sure which way the decision was going to go.

Then, after what seemed like an eternity, the ref brought his whistle to his lips and signalled. It was a goal! Thorgan was right, he *had* timed his run perfectly.

Now Dortmund had the lead – and they had a decision to make. Should they push for a fifth goal to seal their victory, or try to hang on for the win?

Erling didn't know what his team-mates wanted to do, but he had no doubts. He wanted his hat-trick.

He got his moment ten minutes later. Marco Reus slipped Erling in behind Augsburg's high defensive line, with a perfectly-weighted through-ball. Erling was instantly away and bearing down on goal. He could feel the defenders closing in on him, and for a moment it felt as if he was running through treacle.

The ball was stuck under his feet and he couldn't quite get the angles right. The defenders were breathing down his neck now, and he could see the goalkeeper looming in front of him. But he wasn't going to be denied his hat-trick. Not now, not on his debut.

He found an extra burst of strength and speed and

poked the ball with the side of his left foot. It rolled past the keeper and nestled in the back of the net.

He'd done it. He hadn't just scored on his debut – he'd got a hat-trick. Now, everyone in Germany, perhaps everyone in Europe, would be watching him.

"So getting some minutes under your belt wasn't enough for you!" Gio Reyna said with a huge grin.

At full time, Erling went to the ref and took the match ball, a big grin plastered on his face.

"You know it's not a proper hat-trick, right?" the captain, Marco Reus, laughed. "Not in Germany."

"What?" Erling replied.

"You can't have someone scoring in-between your goals," Reus chuckled. "But I'll let you have it this time."

Erling laughed, but kept a tight hold on the match ball.

It was a brilliant start to his Dortmund career, but he'd scored many hat-tricks before and he knew this wouldn't be his last.

This wouldn't be his last big moment for Dortmund, either. Of that he was sure.

2

PHENOMENON

June 2006, Bryne FK Training Ground, Bryne, Norway

"Just imagine you're playing with me and your brother back home," Alf-Inge Haaland said, smiling down at his five-year-old son.

Erling was quiet. It was one thing having a kick-around on the playground at school, or with his brother in the garden, but this was Bryne FK. This wasn't the school team, this was a real football club.

But this wasn't *any* football club – this was a Norwegian team with an incredible history. Bryne FK had qualified for Europe, they'd finished in the top two multiple times and – most important of all – this was the club where Erling's dad had begun his career.

Erling could already sense the other kids looking at him – or more likely, looking at his dad. He knew they all recognised Alfie Haaland, and they knew that Erling was his son. He knew that the kids would expect something from him. They'd expect him to live up to that name.

"They already know who I am, Dad," Erling said.

"Don't worry about that, son. Just be yourself. The most important thing today is that you have a good time."

Out of the corner of his eye, Erling noticed a man approaching them. Despite the fact that they were indoors, he was wrapped up tight in a big coat and a thick scarf.

He stretched out a hand towards Erling's father.

"Alfie," he chuckled. "It's good to see you back here again. Brings back memories, eh?"

Erling's dad laughed and the two chatted happily for a few moments.

"And this must be little Erling, huh?" the man said, glancing down and sticking out a hand, "I'm Alf Ingve Berntsen. I'm the youth coach here."

Erling took his hand and shook it, not sure what to say.

"I know you're new here, Erling, but we're going to put you with the team a year above your age group," Alf Ingve continued. "We play mixed teams here – boys and girls – but if you're half as good as your dad tells me, you'll be fine."

With an arm around Erling's shoulder, Alf Ingve led the boy over to a pitch in the corner of the arena.

Erling could feel the eyes of everyone boring into him. They wanted to see what Alf-Inge's son was made of. But it didn't faze him. He just wanted to get going, feel the ball at his feet.

"Where do you normally play, then?" Alf Ingve asked him as they stood on the touchline. The match was already underway and Erling watched the mob of kids chasing each other across the pitch.

"Striker," he replied.

"Well, let's hope you're a better goalscorer than your dad," Alf Ingve chuckled.

A minute later, Erling was on the pitch. He could feel the players all focusing their gaze on him. They were eager to see if Haaland's son was any good.

It took a while for him to adjust to the game. His legs felt heavy and it was difficult to run, but gradually he started to get the rhythm of the game.

"Else!" he roared, as one of his team-mates dribbled forward with the ball. "To me!"

She passed the ball into him and he controlled it deftly with the inside of his left foot. He felt a defender closing him down and he faked to go to the left. As the defender moved that way, Erling was already moving down the right-hand side.

A second defender was already coming towards him and he accelerated past, bursting into the box. He twisted his body, wrapping his left foot around the ball, aiming to curl it into the far corner.

It worked exactly as he intended, and he watched the ball sail past the keeper and into the bottom of the goal.

Arms outstretched, he wheeled around in celebration.

"Wow! What a goal," Else told him.

"Thanks. Nice assist, too!" Erling replied.

"Great goal, Erling," Alf Ingve called from the sidelines. Erling looked to his dad, who gave him a small thumbs-up.

The goal gave Erling more confidence and his nervousness slowly fell away. Feeling more comfortable with the ball at his feet, he started trying new things. He was shooting from distance, running at defenders and trying little skills and flicks.

Once more, Else picked up the ball on the right wing and Erling moved into position in the box. He raised his arm high, instead of shouting and revealing his position to the defender.

Else went to pass the ball, but she miskicked it and it flew into the air. The other players moved towards where it was going to land, but Erling moved directly towards the ball and leapt into the air. His head met with the ball, powering it towards the goal, where it nestled in the back of the net.

GOAL!

Erling's team-mates all congratulated him, even more impressed with this goal than his first. Already, he'd earned their respect. To them, he was no longer "Alfie Haaland's son". He was Erling.

Too soon for his liking, the game was over and both teams trudged off the pitch. As Erling walked over to his dad, Alf Ingve Berntsen caught up with him, a huge grin on his face.

"Amazing, Erling! Just amazing!" he said. "The way you jumped for that second one – you must have the biggest leap of any five-year-old! I think you've got a big future here at Bryne!"

"Thank you," Erling mumbled, as he carried on walking over to his dad.

"Keep this up and you'll be the best Haaland ever to have played!" Alf Ingve shouted after him.

3

WALKING TALL

July 2014, Bryne FK Training Ground, Bryne, Norway

"Who are you and what have you done with Erling?" Alf Ingve bellowed, as Erling jogged towards him across the pitch.

"It's just a little growth spurt," Erling laughed, shrugging and looking down at his long body.

In the ten years since Erling had first impressed Alf Ingve, he'd progressed through Bryne's youth teams with ease, but he'd still been waiting for the growth spurt that would allow him to kick on with his football career.

His dad had been a big, tough, tackling defender and his mum a talented heptathlete. Even Erling's older brother was a good head taller than him. Erling had known his time would come, but the longer he had had to wait, the less likely it had seemed.

He'd kept expecting to wake up one morning and find himself suddenly six foot-four, with huge muscles. But for months, he'd woken up every morning disappointed.

"It's better to develop later," Alf Ingve had kept telling him. "When you're smaller you can develop your technical skills – you won't be reliant on your physical size. It's better this way."

Erling knew that Alf Ingve was right, but he couldn't help being frustrated. All too often he'd knock the ball in front of him and sprint after it, only to be overtaken by a much taller defender.

In the end, it had been a gradual process that Erling hadn't even noticed was happening. By the end of July, he stood at over six feet tall.

"So, are you ready for today's session?" Alf Ingve asked, looking up and down at Erling.

Erling nodded, looking past Alf Ingve to where a few of the other players were warming up.

"We'll have you training with the first team soon," Alf Ingve continued, as they walked over to the training pitch.

"Really? Isn't it a bit early?" Erling asked.

"There's only so far we can take you at Bryne, Erling," Alf Ingve admitted. "I'm sure you'll outgrow us soon."

Erling didn't answer. He loved everything at Bryne – the town, his coaches, his team-mates. After growing up with the same group of players over the past ten years, many of them had become Erling's best friends.

But his dad had moved to England at the age of 22, and Erling knew he couldn't stay in Norway if he wanted to make it at the highest level.

"Anyway, that's for another time," Alf Ingve said, breaking the silence. "Let's focus on today and see what you can do with this new height of yours."

The session was a tough one. It may have been summer in Norway, but it was a bitterly cold day and the rain was falling. Alf Ingve and the other coaches guided the players through a few basic drills, before finally getting to what they were all waiting for – a match.

Even though it was only a training match between team-mates, Erling didn't like losing. From a young age, his dad had instilled in him a fierce winning mentality. It was win at all costs, no matter the situation.

"I don't mean losing the game," Alfie had told his son. "You don't want to come off the pitch knowing that you didn't put everything you possibly could into a match. If you haven't put in a hundred per cent, you've lost."

That was in Erling's mind as the training match began. He was going to show everyone what he could do.

Right at the beginning of the match, Erling flew into a crunching challenge with Morten, an opposing player.

"Easy, Erling," he said.

"Sorry, mate," Erling replied, pulling Morten back up to his feet. "I didn't realise how fast I was going!"

Moments later, he had his first chance. He brushed

off a defender and swivelled, getting the ball onto his left foot. Now there was space in front of him, and he smashed the ball forward. He sprinted after it, his feet pounding the floor.

For once, his feet seemed to obey him. There was no defender anywhere near him and he was almost caught off guard when he caught up to the ball before it had stopped moving. He had to stop suddenly and slow down to get the ball under control. Then he hammered the ball towards the top-left corner of the goal, giving the keeper no chance.

He added a second with a powerful header from a corner. And then, before the game came to an end, he completed his hat-trick. A ball over the top left the defenders stranded and Erling quickly outpaced them. He was clear and just facing down the keeper.

He faked to go left onto his stronger left foot, but then threw in a stepover, before going right and leaving the keeper stranded on the turf. All he had to do was tap the ball into the empty net.

"Come on, Erling! It's only a friendly!" someone shouted.

"You can't embarrass me like that!" the keeper laughed, getting back to his feet.

The end of the match marked the end of the training session, but Erling didn't feel tired. As everyone else headed off to the changing rooms, Erling decided to stay for some extra shooting practice.

"That new height of yours seems to be treating you well, Erling. Amazing game," Alf Ingve said, as Erling set out some cones for his drills. "If you keep that up, we're going to have you in the first team quicker than we thought. You'll be taller than some of them too!"

4
FIRST-TEAM DEBUT

May 2016, Extra Arena, Ranheim, Norway
Ranheim Fotball v Bryne FK

"What's going on?" Erling asked the team's captain, Bjørnar Holmvik.

"The gaffer's been sacked," Bjørnar replied, tapping furiously on his phone. "I'm just trying to find out who's replacing him. They think it might be Alf."

Boosted by his new height, Erling's football had gone to another level. The technical skills he'd developed when he was smaller were now secondary to his speed and strength.

At the beginning of the 2015/16 season, he'd been promoted into Bryne's second team, playing in Norway's fourth division. It was a significant step up from playing against youth teams. The defenders were far more physical and Erling often left the pitch with bruises on his ankles.

But his new-found size meant he gave as good as he got, and he was racking up the goals, scoring 18 times in just 14 appearances. He was knocking on the door of the first team, and he just needed an opportunity to get in and show what he could do.

During a training session with the reserves, Erling had spotted the commotion on the other side of the training field when the first-team manager, Gaute Larsen, had been sacked.

It was a big shock for Erling to hear that Alf Ingve Berntsen, the man who'd coached him since the age of five, was in the frame to be named as Bryne's new first-team manager. Under Berntsen, Erling knew he had a better chance of being called up to the first team.

"No matter who the new manager is, you've got to be patient, Erling," his dad told him. "I don't know any other players who made their first-team debut at 15. Even in five years' time, you'll still be a young player. There's no need to rush."

"But I want to play in the Premier League like you!" Erling replied. "I want to be one of the best players in the world. If I can do this, then I can do anything."

"Alright, alright," Alf-Inge accepted. "You have to be ready to take your chance, then. Don't be intimidated or scared to stand up for yourself."

A few days later, Alf Ingve was formally appointed as temporary manager and he included Erling in his first match-day squad, for an away game against Ranheim. Erling was starting on the bench, but the manager had told him he'd try to get him on.

The hosts were a few places above Bryne in the table, so it was a good opportunity for the team to grab some important points.

Alf Ingve caught up with Erling as the players left the changing room.

"I'll try and get you on in the second half," he said.

"Just relax and play your natural game, see what you can do. Don't worry – you'll be fine!"

"I'm sure I will," Erling replied with a smirk.

"Oh yeah, I forgot – you're not like normal players," Alf Ingve laughed, shaking his head.

The first half was quiet, except for an early penalty for Ranheim, which they converted. Bryne now had to find a way back into the match and, twenty minutes into the second half, they turned to their 15-year-old striker.

Erling had been pacing up and down the touchline, occasionally bursting into a light jog, as if he was warming up. He was itching to get on the pitch, desperate to show what he could do.

He replaced Robert Undheim and went on out wide, instead of in his usual striker role. It wasn't where he felt natural, but he knew that, even from there, he could make a difference.

Erling chased down every ball and competed for every header as Bryne desperately pumped balls forward, chasing an equaliser. If he thought the step-up to the reserves had been hard, this was another level.

The defenders were that little bit sharper, that little bit stronger and smarter. They were quicker to every ball and Erling felt himself battered, each time getting to the ball slightly too late.

But he grew into the game, slowly getting a few touches, and he even had a shot that was blocked by a Ranheim defender.

Then, before he knew it, the game was over. He hadn't made the amazing start to his professional football career that he'd wanted, but it was a start.

And with Alf Ingve in charge, he knew that this was just the beginning. He'd be playing more senior-level matches in no time.

5

MEETING A LEGEND

February 2017, Molde Training Ground, Molde, Norway

"They're a big club, Erling. Your career could really take off there. The Bundesliga is a top league."

"It's not the Premier League though, is it?"

"You're years younger than I was when I moved to England to join Nottingham Forest. But times have changed – you don't know when an opportunity like this is going to come around again."

After playing 16 matches for Bryne without scoring a goal, Erling felt only disappointment. He was still being played as a winger, which he thought was a waste of his talents.

But his performances hadn't gone unnoticed and the mid-table German Bundesliga club, Hoffenheim, had offered him a trial. And, because Erling was still only 15, he hadn't signed a professional contract, so was free to sign with any club that wanted him.

After taking a few days to think about it, Erling finally decided to turn the offer down. It was only a trial, and there were no guarantees that he'd get signed up. And even if he was, he knew that it could be years before he'd be playing for the first team.

He decided instead to continue training with Bryne, putting all his effort into their training sessions. If he was going to remain at Bryne, he was going to make sure that he kept his place in their first team. After all, he was still desperate to get his first professional goal.

When Erling was in the dressing room after one training session, his dad called him.

"You won't believe who I've just been talking to,"

Alf-Inge blurted out. "Does the name Ole Gunnar Solskjær mean anything to you?"

Of course Erling knew who Ole Gunnar Solskjær was. He was the legendary former Norwegian striker who'd won the Champions League with Man United. He was currently the manager of Molde, one of Norway's biggest teams.

"Wait – Molde want me?" Erling asked, getting straight down to the important business. If there was an opportunity to move to Molde and play under Norway's greatest-ever striker, then it was a no-brainer. He had to make that transfer.

Once his dad had confirmed the interest, the rest was little more than a formality. By the end of February, Erling was training with Molde. He finally got to meet his hero, Ole.

Ole wasn't a big man, but he completely dominated every room he was in. Especially here in Norway, where he had such a reputation. Captivated, Erling was desperate to soak up every bit of advice he could from the manager. If anyone knew about goalscoring, it was Ole.

His first little tip had come just a couple of weeks into Erling's fledgling Molde career.

"You move too much, Erling," Ole shouted over to him, gesturing the young player over. Ole strode onto the pitch and took Erling's place in the drill they were running. Erling had been moving all over the place, trying to find space so he could bring the ball down from the corner.

He watched now as Ole took his place in the box. The ball was floated in and Ole didn't seem to move. As it was flicked on by one of the other strikers, Erling felt his eyes drawn to the ball and away from Ole. But as the ball moved across the box, suddenly it was Ole who was there, tapping it past the keeper from close range.

"You see what I did, Erling?" he asked, turning back to where Erling was standing.

"It's not about moving all the time," he continued. "You have to be clever with your movement – wait for the right time. Again!"

They repeated the drill a few times and, although it was for the whole team, it felt as if Erling had been singled out, as if he was getting a personal lesson from Ole Gunnar Solskjær.

He couldn't believe how lucky he was. If only the lads from Bryne could see him now ...

It was then Erling's turn to step in. The ball came across and he moved slowly behind the defenders, before launching himself in the air to win the header. As the defenders bounced off him and landed on the floor, Erling met the ball with his head – but it cannoned a long way over the bar.

"Come on, Erling mate!" one of the defenders roared up at him. "There's no need for that."

"Let's go again," Erling replied, hauling the players to their feet.

6
OFF THE MARK

April 2017, Volda Stadion, Volda, Møre og Romsdal, Norway
Volda TI v Molde FK

"I know this isn't the kind of stadium we're used to, lads, but it's important that we stay focused. We've got a real chance of winning this cup – and that all starts today!" Solskjær stood in the dressing room and looked around at his players.

Erling had always thought that Bryne played in a small stadium, but it was nothing compared to Volda's ground. The home team played in the third division, and there were barely any seats for fans to sit in.

Erling had watched Molde's opening games of the season from the bench. The manager hadn't been ready to risk him yet, but after training with Molde for a few months, Erling was ready to make his debut.

And today, Ole was ready to risk him.

He caught up with Erling before he left the dressing room.

"You've got something I never had, Erling," he told him. "You're tall, you're strong, you're fast ... Don't be afraid to use that. Put yourself about a bit. There's goals for you out there!"

The first half was a quiet and drab affair. Erling had a couple of opportunities, but he wasn't quite able to get behind the Volda defence. It wasn't until the second half that he got his first real chance.

A good pass from Thomas Amang was inch-perfect, allowing Erling to continue his run. He got the ball out and moved forward into the box. The pitch was poor and the ball bobbled and bounced in front of him – he had to concentrate, making sure he didn't slice it.

Eventually he was able to fire a shot towards goal, using the bobble of the pitch to help it bounce over the keeper. The ball trickled slowly towards the goal-line, where a defender attempting a block could only deflect it into the top of the goal.

It wasn't the cleanest strike, and it certainly wasn't one of his best goals, but that didn't matter.

"I'm having that one!" Erling roared, raising his arm in triumph, as his team-mates all clambered around him, celebrating his first professional goal.

"Scoring at 16? I think my first professional goal was ten years after that," one of Erling's team-mates joked.

At the final whistle, Ole ran over to hug his young striker.

"I'm proud of you, Erling. If you're scoring goals now, imagine how many more you've got to come!"

7

IMPACT SUB

September 2017, SR Bank Arena, Stavanger, Norway
Viking FK v Molde FK

"Erling! Get ready! You're coming on!"

It was a shout that Erling had become increasingly used to over the last couple of months. Quickly, he hurried back to the half-way line, cutting short his warm-up.

After the goal against Volda on his debut, Erling had half-expected to go straight into the starting line-up. But it hadn't been the case. He'd spent most games watching from the bench, just occasionally being summoned on as a late sub – and being asked to do a lot in the final minutes of the game.

It was a role that Erling hated. How was he supposed to impact the game and impress the manager in ten minutes or so?

He'd voiced his concerns to his dad, who'd listened politely at first, but Erling could sense that eventually he'd grown tired of Erling's moaning.

"Erling, you're not 17 for another month," Alf-Inge had told him, his tone measured but firm. "I didn't make my debut until I was 18. Ole didn't sign for Molde until he was in his twenties. I know you're desperate to be a part of the team, but you have to be patient."

"I know all that, Dad, but it's hard to be patient when I'm good enough to improve the team!" Erling complained. "I'm not being greedy – I *know* I can make a difference. But how can I do that, playing ten minutes every other week?"

His dad had sighed. He knew his son better than anyone. After all, it was Alf-Inge who had instilled that drive, that winning mentality into his son. It was he who'd pushed him at every turn, filling him with stories of his time at Leeds and Man City. He only had himself to blame for having a son who was so determined, so difficult.

"Look, I get it, Erling," he'd continued, "and so will Ole. We've both been subs in our careers, we've both wanted to play games and get in the side."

"Yeah, I guess," Erling had admitted. He sometimes forgot that other people had been through the same thing as him. Sometimes it felt as if he was the only person in the world that this was happening to.

But it was helpful to hear it in perspective – and deep down, he knew his dad was right. Erling often felt that he was stalling, his career going backwards, but in truth he wasn't even 17 yet, and he was already playing for Molde in the top level of Norwegian football. How many other 16-year-olds were doing that?

"If you want to know about making an impact off the bench, speak to Ole," his dad added. "His record coming off the bench for United was incredible. If anyone knows about making a difference from the bench, it's him."

Erling took his dad's advice and, in the very next training session, he nervously approached Ole.

"I know I'm probably going to be coming on from the bench for a bit," he said apprehensively. "So I want to know how to make an impact in the time I'll have on the pitch. Like you used to do at United."

"Did your dad put you up to this?" Ole laughed, perhaps sensing that asking for advice wasn't Erling's usual style.

Erling nodded, laughing along with Ole and feeling a little more at ease.

"The trick is to not spend too much time thinking about yourself," Ole explained. "When I was on the bench, I watched the defenders, looking for their weaknesses."

Erling nodded, making mental notes.

"If you do that, then by the time you get on the pitch you'll know the strengths and weaknesses of the centre-backs. You won't need to spend five minutes adjusting to the game, because you'll already know who's fast, who's strong, who's a sloppy passer. You get the idea?"

"Is that what you did in '99?" Erling asked, talking about the 1999 Champions League final against Bayern

Munich, when, after coming on as a sub, Ole had scored the winner for Man United.

"No, that was all luck!" Ole laughed. "But what I'm telling you works. Try it in the next game and see if you can make it work for you."

That "next game" was today. Once more, Erling had found himself on the bench and, once more, he was being put on with 25 minutes left to play.

Molde were away at Viking and they were leading 2-1, with the opposition down to 10 men. It was the perfect setup for Erling to come on and try to get some goals.

He'd spent his time on the bench closely watching the Viking players. Their number two, Martinsen, had looked uncomfortable since they'd gone down to 10 men. If Erling could get in behind him, he knew he would find space. There would be chances for him.

Not long after Erling came on, Viking got a shock equaliser, to level the game at 2-2. It was clear they were going to sit deep now and space was going to be limited for Erling and the other Molde strikers. He would need to take his chances when they came.

With 10 minutes left to play, Molde got their chance. A ball was knocked over the top towards Fredrik Aursnes, and both he and Erling sprinted forward. Erling held back, lurking in Martinsen's blind spot.

The defender went racing across to close down Aursnes, leaving Erling in acres of space.

"Fred!" he roared, "Square it!"

The ball was good, but it bobbled and bounced over the pitch. Erling took a slight breath to compose himself. He couldn't afford to swing at this wildly and end up blasting it over.

Carefully, he pulled his left foot back and slotted the ball past the keeper.

"Come on!" he bellowed, as the Molde fans who'd travelled for the game celebrated wildly. Erling had not just made an impact from the bench – he'd got the winner.

"So you *were* listening in training the other day!" Ole grinned, after the final whistle. "You keep making the most of those opportunities and I'm going to have a hard time leaving you out of the starting line-up!"

8
FOUR IN TWENTY

July 2018, Brann Stadion, Bergen, Norway
SK Brann v Molde FK

"You're my main guy now, Erling. We want to win the league – and I want you at the centre of it," Ole told him at the start of the season.

Erling's goal against Viking hadn't catapulted him into the starting line-up, but it had given him far more confidence. He could now make a difference from the bench, even if it was only in ten or fifteen minutes.

Then, heading into the 2018 Eliteserien season, Molde's main striker, Björn Sigurðarson, had departed the club, and Ole had made it clear to the players that there would be no replacement coming in.

It was the first time in Erling's career that he'd been assured of his place in the team. He couldn't be sure that Ole would follow through with his promise, but he was confident. He trusted Ole to deliver – and he knew that, even if he didn't, Erling would find a way to force his way into the team.

Molde had started the season well, and Erling was happy that he could focus on what the team was doing, rather than on his own personal quest to get into the team.

Although they'd finished a distant second a couple of times, Molde hadn't won the league title since 2014. Yet this year somehow felt different, and Erling was sure they could win it.

Perhaps it was just because he was now established in the team, but there seemed to be a better atmosphere around the club. Ole was full of smiles and the players were full of confidence, feeding off his optimism.

The game today was a big one. Molde were away at the current leaders, SK Brann. They were the on-form team in the division, unbeaten all season. If Molde were serious about their title credentials, then they needed to win today.

Erling was starting up front, supported by wingers Petter Strand and Eirik Hestad. Despite Ole's confidence and Molde's decent form, Erling had been struggling for goals, only scoring twice so far in the 2018 season.

Before kick-off, Ole beckoned his young striker over in the changing room.

"I've got faith in you today, Erling," Ole told him. "I know you've struggled a bit for goals, and I know how frustrating that is, but – trust me – you're getting in all the right places. The goals will come, for sure."

Erling nodded. He knew that he was going to get chances and he knew that he was going to finish them. So why not today? Why not against top-of-the-league Brann? It was as good a game as any.

Even though he was starting the game, Erling continued to follow the advice that Ole had given him when he was coming off the bench. So Erling spent the first couple of minutes watching the opposition players, jogging between the centre-backs, testing out their speed and strength.

"Erling!" Fredrik Aursnes shouted to him, running over. "We've played this team before," he said. "Their keeper comes rushing out early, to sweep up behind the defence. If we get a pass over the top and you run onto it, you'll get a chance!"

Just four minutes into the first half, Aursnes was proved right. A ball was lofted over the top and Aursnes rose to flick it on. As soon as the ball was in the air, Erling was moving, keeping himself onside but evading the defenders.

Erling had already spotted the keeper coming off his line and he knew he was going to beat him. He was quicker than the keeper and the defenders. His first touch with his right foot took him past the keeper and wide to the right of the box.

He didn't even need to look at where the goal was. He struck the ball immediately with his left foot and it flew into the back of the net.

The home fans were stunned into silence, as the small

number of Molde fans cheered their team's quick start. Erling picked out Fredrik Aursnes in the celebrations.

"Great shout, Fred!" he yelled.

"I told you, didn't I?" Fredrik replied with a wide grin.

It was still only four minutes in and already Molde were one-up against the league leaders. But, more important, Erling had ended his goal drought – and he wasn't done yet. He could sense there were more goals for him in this game.

Brann had the ball now and had started to dominate possession. Erling spent a lot of the next ten minutes watching the game from the far end of the pitch, but he wasn't worried. He knew that if Molde got the ball to him quickly, he could make a difference. There was space in this game.

Eirik Hestad did just that, looping a long ball forward. Erling chased after it, getting there first and finding himself one-on-one with just a single Brann defender. He flicked the ball round him, cleverly darting round the other side of the player and collecting the ball behind him.

Now, he was in on goal and there was no chance of

them stopping him. He bore down and slotted the ball under the onrushing keeper.

Molde were 2-0 up – and they'd played barely 15 minutes!

"That was genius, Erling!" Eirik shouted, when he caught up with Erling. "I've got no idea how you did that bit of skill!"

"Neither do I," Erling shrugged, laughing. "Thanks for the assist too."

A couple of minutes later, Erling got his next chance. A sloppy mistake at the back allowed the ball to bounce through. There was a vast amount of space in behind for Erling to run into, and he chased after the ball.

Once more, the keeper came charging out and, once more, Erling was too quick for him. He flicked the ball round him with his left foot and then hit it first-time, again with his left, then watched the ball roll into the back of the vacant net.

Erling turned and jogged away towards the fans. He almost didn't know what to do. After waiting and fighting for so long to get into the team, and after finding goals difficult to come by, he'd just scored a hat-trick against the league leaders. And not just *any* hat-trick. He'd scored all three goals in just 15 minutes.

"If you continue at this rate you'll score 10 today!" Fredrik Aursnes laughed, as he joined the celebrations.

"There's still a long way to go," Erling reminded him. "We don't want them to get a sniff of our goal."

Five minutes later, Eirik Hestad was fouled in the box and Molde were awarded a penalty.

"I'm having it!" Erling bellowed, grabbing the ball. With the form he was in, nobody was going to argue with him, even if he was only a teenager.

Erling stood in front of the ball, breathing deeply. Then he sprinted forward, pausing slightly before the ball, and rolled it into the bottom of the net.

He had sealed victory against the league leaders – but, more importantly for Erling, it had put him on the map in Norway.

Tomorrow, everyone would know his name – the kid who'd scored four times in 20 minutes.

9

A TASTE OF EUROPE

August 2018, Aker Stadion, Molde, Norway
Molde FK v Hibernian FC

"This is only Round Three of qualifying, lads," Ole told the players before the game. "If we get through this, we'll only be a couple of wins away from the group stage, taking on the likes of Arsenal or Chelsea!"

Erling had spent his childhood watching players like Ronaldinho, Messi and Cristiano Ronaldo on TV, dominating games in the Champions League. They had been entertaining, exciting players to watch – and, more importantly, they had won games. Ever since, Erling had been desperate to play in that competition, to play against the best of the best from all over Europe.

And although he wasn't playing in the Champions League yet – this was only the Europa League – he was still excited. Tonight was only his third game in Europe, and he'd already got his first UEFA goal, with a penalty against KF Laçi in the last qualifying round.

Tonight he was keen to get his first goal from open play.

He'd missed the first leg, where Molde had played a hard-fought 0-0 draw with the Scottish side, Hibernian. Molde were in a good position to get through if they won today, but it wasn't going to be easy. An away goal for Hibs would put them in the driving seat.

"If you could get another four goals today, Erling, that would be nice!" Eirik Hestad called over to him, as they warmed up for the game.

"I'll give it my best shot," Erling grinned. He was only half-joking – getting four goals in the Europa League, even if it was against a team like Hibernian, would definitely put him on the European map. And it didn't seem that far-fetched. He'd watched Hibernian defend in that first leg – there were goals for him here.

He got his first goal after barely 35 minutes. A looped free kick was headed towards goal by the captain, Ruben Gabrielsen. There were a couple of Hibs defenders on the line and, fearing it was going to be cleared, Erling threw himself at the ball, nodding it into the back of the net.

"Sorry!" Erling shouted to his captain. "I had to make sure!"

It was his first goal from open play in the Europa League, but it wasn't the goal he wanted. That one wasn't going to make headlines. It wasn't a goal to put him in the same bracket as some of the best players in Europe.

Erling was involved in Molde's second goal, racing clear and flicking the ball back to Fredrik Aursnes, who tucked it into the empty net.

"That's the first time you've ever set *me* up," Aursnes laughed.

"That's the first time I was confident you'd score,"

Erling joked. "Even you couldn't miss an open goal like that!"

The Molde team were in a buoyant mood now, and Erling was at the centre of it. He normally spent most of his games on the fringes, only getting the ball when he was racing clear. But tonight he was involved in everything Molde were doing. He was spraying passes across the pitch, shrugging off defenders and whipping in crosses. The only thing he needed now was another goal.

Ten minutes from the end, he got it. Magnus Wolff Eikrem's shot deflected off the defender and flew into the air. Erling was the first to react, controlling it, rounding the keeper and tucking it home.

Molde were now 3-0 up and sailing into the next round of Europa League qualifying. Erling had been at the heart of everything good they'd done.

He was more than just their striker now, he was their talisman – and he couldn't wait to add more goals in Europe.

10
NEW HORIZONS

August 2018, Erling's House, Molde, Norway

"You were brilliant, Erling!" Alf-Inge said with a wide smile, as he hugged his son.

"I just hope we can go a bit further," Erling said. "I want to get into the group stages."

"Well, let's put that on hold for a little bit," his dad added, a wry smile on his face.

It was the same look he'd had when he'd told

Erling about the interest from Molde and Ole Gunnar Solskjær.

"What is it, Dad?" Erling asked, sitting up.

"Well – we've got a couple of offers on the table."

Erling had been aware that the summer transfer window was open, and he'd had half an eye on the transfer rumours that were circulating on the internet. He knew that his goalscoring exploits against Brann had put him in the public eye, but he hadn't really expected anything to happen. After all, he'd only had one full season at Molde – surely that wasn't enough to generate a big move?

"So, we've got an offer from my old club, Leeds," Alf-Inge continued. "And we've got one from Red Bull Salzburg, out in Austria."

Erling hesitated. For so long, it had been his dream to go and play in England one day, just as his dad had done. Leeds might not be in the Premier League, but they were in England – and they were the team that his dad had played for, all those years ago.

"What are you thinking, Erling?" his dad asked, breaking the silence.

"I'm not sure," Erling replied. "I really want to play for Leeds, but it doesn't feel right. It feels too soon."

His dad nodded. "Normally I'd be desperate for you to go to Leeds, but … at Salzburg, you'll have the chance to win the league, you'll probably get to play in the Champions League – and they've got connections with so many clubs across Europe."

Erling realised that his dad was right. He knew that players like Sadio Mané had developed at Salzburg and had gone on to have big careers in Europe. It didn't feel like the exciting choice or the emotional one, but it was the logical one. Erling knew it was the right one.

The transfer was agreed in the summer of 2018, but Erling didn't get to join Red Bull Salzburg until January of 2019.

It actually worked out well for him. By then, the Norwegian season had finished, so Erling had time to adapt to his new life in Austria, without the pressure of having to play games every week.

On a bitterly cold January morning, Erling took part in his first Salzburg training session. The weather was familiar, but the session was in stark contrast to what he was used to back in Norway.

"Energy, lads! Close him down! Press him!" Marco Rose, Salzburg's manager, shouted. Salzburg defended more aggressively than most other teams.

"You'll need to work hard if you want to play in my team," Rose said to Erling during the session. "Show a bit of hunger when the ball comes towards you. You need to be ready to go!"

In the match at the end of the session, the speed of play was higher than any game Erling had played in before. The ball flew past him several times and he found himself sprinting almost aimlessly around the pitch, chasing shadows. It was five minutes before he got a touch – and he was immediately clattered by Stefan Lainer. The Austrian won the ball with ease and raced away.

Erling had always been a strong player, but he wasn't used to being beaten to the ball like that. Yet, despite his frustration, as he got to his feet he had a smile on his face.

He was in the right place. Here, he would become a better player.

11
THE RIGHT CHOICE

May 2019, Red Bull Arena, Salzburg, Austria
FC Red Bull Salzburg v LASK

"The title is in the bag, boys," Marco Rose told his players, "but LASK are still our rivals. So let's go out there and show them why we're the best team in Austria!"

After months of training with his new team, and making a few sub appearances, Erling was yet to start a game.

But today, with the league title all but wrapped up,

the boss was giving some of his younger players a chance to impress, in a home game against LASK.

Erling was starting up-front in Salzburg's 4-4-2, alongside fellow Norwegian, Fredrik Gulbrandsen.

"Don't be too nervous, alright Erling?" Gulbrandsen murmured to him as they came onto the pitch. "We've got nothing to lose today! Let's have some fun and get a few goals!"

"I'm not nervous," Erling laughed. He wasn't trying to impress his new team-mate – it was just that he didn't feel nervous at all. He felt excitement – he was desperate to get out on the pitch and score, to test himself against the best. And LASK were one of the best in Austria.

For the first 10 minutes LASK showed their class. Their back-three were experienced, strong and well-organised. They competed with Erling on a physical level and gave him little space in which he could control the ball and turn.

Then, as full-back Patrick Farkas picked up the ball, Erling spotted his chance.

"Pat! Over the top!" he shouted, curving his run to keep him onside.

The ball was perfect and Erling found himself with acres of space as the keeper came out. He didn't need to think – he just hit it first time. It wasn't the smoothest strike and it wasn't quite what he intended, but it was enough. It was a goal.

It was Erling's first goal for Red Bull Salzburg – and, to make it sweeter, he'd got it on his first start as well.

As he ran off in celebration, pursued by his team-mates, and with the home fans in the Red Bull Arena all cheering his name, he couldn't help but think about that decision last year.

Salzburg or Leeds?

He knew he'd made the right choice.

12

3 X 3

May 2019, Lublin Stadium, Lublin, Poland
Norway U20 v Honduras U20

"A big win today and we still have a chance of qualifying!" The Norway U20 manager, Pål Arne Johansen stood in front of his players, attempting to fire them up.

It was the first time that Norway had qualified for the U20 World Cup in over 25 years, but so far the tournament had been a major disappointment. They had lost their first two games, against New Zealand and Uruguay, which meant that they needed to get a good result here to be in with a chance of qualifying for the last 16.

Erling hadn't been convinced that he wanted to play at the U20 World Cup. It had meant that he'd missed the end of the Austrian season, and he was worried that if he got injured, he wouldn't be able to keep his place in the Salzburg side.

It was only his dad's words that had convinced him he needed to go.

"Do you want to be one of those players that prioritises their club over their country?" he'd asked.

"It's only the under-20 … " Erling began.

"It's Norway. Do you think Ronaldo prefers Real Madrid or Portugal? Do you think Messi prefers Barcelona or Argentina?"

Erling shrugged.

"They play well for both," his dad continued. "Do you want to be one of the best in the world? You need to be willing to put a hundred per cent effort into everything – for club *and* for country. If you give up on this tournament now, you'll be setting the tone for the rest of your career."

At first, Erling thought that his dad was being harsh, but perhaps he was right. After all, Erling's aim had always been to be one of the very best in *world* football, not one of the best in *club* football.

So, with that in mind, he had accepted the call to join Norway's U20 squad. And here he was, lining up against Honduras on a hot summer's day in Poland.

"We can get a few today," winger Jens Petter Hauge said to Erling, as they lined up.

"You just give me the ball and I'll get us the goals," Erling replied.

Honduras had been the worst team in the group so far and, with goal difference on the line, the Norwegians were confident that they could get the goals they needed to get qualification. Erling hadn't scored in either of Norway's first two games, so he was particularly keen to make his mark.

Now he was here, he was determined not to waste this tournament. And that meant getting goals.

His first came after just seven minutes. Hauge flicked

the ball into the box and, with the Honduras keeper floundering, Erling had the simplest of tasks to tap it into the back of the net.

"I told you!" Erling shouted. "Just give me the ball and I'll do the rest!"

"I did all of that!" Hauge protested. "You didn't do anything!"

Erling's second came inside 20 minutes. A brilliant ball from Tobias Børkeeiet landed perfectly at Erling's feet. He knocked it on and then drilled it hard and low between the legs of the Honduras keeper.

Barely 10 minutes later, Erling had his hat-trick. He was hacked down in the box by the keeper, after being played through. It was a clear penalty and there was only one man who was going to take it.

Erling stepped up and fired the ball carefully into the bottom corner.

"You could get ten if you carry on at this rate!" Hauge roared, as they celebrated the goal.

Hauge was joking, but Erling could sense that something was going to happen. There was an atmosphere in the ground today.

He had the scent of goals now – and he wasn't going to stop.

Just before half-time, he added his fourth – Norway's fifth – and once again it was Hauge who set him up. He flicked a ball into Erling, who controlled it, let it bounce, and then hammered it into the top corner.

At half-time, Norway were 5-0 up, and Erling had four of them.

Jens Petter Hauge got a goal early in the second half, but then Erling took over once more.

For the third time, he was set up by Hauge. The winger flicked the ball into Erling, who was bursting into the box. He shrugged off the defenders and drove the ball hard under the keeper and into the net.

Now he had five!

"Take it easy, Erling," Leo Østigård said to him, as they celebrated. "I think we've got the game won."

"I've got some more goals to get," Erling grunted.

With 23 minutes left, Erling got his sixth goal. Kristian Thorstvedt scrambled the ball into the box and Erling was able to wrap his foot around it and somehow direct it into the goal.

"What do you even call that?" Kristian Thorstvedt asked him. "A double hat-trick?"

Erling shrugged. When he was younger, he'd scored five or six in a single match, but this was a real game – and at a major tournament too. This kind of thing wasn't supposed to happen at this level.

And there were still 20 minutes left.

Ten minutes later, Erling added his seventh. A great cross from Håkon Evjen landed at his feet, and he flicked it past the keeper and into the goal.

Erling pumped his fist and grinned at the small section of Norwegian fans in the stadium. They were all chanting his name and cheering him on.

"You'd better stop scoring, Erling," Hauge laughed. "We're running out of ways to celebrate!"

Eman Markovic added a tenth goal for Norway, and then Erling stepped in again.

With two minutes left, he took a pass from Håkon Evjen, burst into the box and smashed it past the keeper.

And then, on the 90-minute mark, he nicked the ball off the feet of Jens Petter Hauge and blasted it high into the net.

"You could have let me have that one!" his team-mate said, shaking his head. "You've got eight goals already, but you were so desperate to get another you had to nick the ball off me?"

"I saw the opportunity," Erling laughed.

It was true. For Erling, as soon as he got into the box, the only thing on his mind was getting the ball into the net as quickly as possible. Nothing else mattered.

They didn't know if Norway were through, but this 12-0 win gave them as good a chance as any.

And Erling?

He'd scored nine goals for his country in a single match. Three hat-tricks. There weren't words to describe that number of goals in a single game.

As Erling walked off the pitch, a member of Norway's backroom staff ran up to him, waving his phone in Erling's face.

"You're already going viral!" he shouted. "Everybody's talking about Erling Haaland!"

13
GOAL MACHINE

August 2019, Red Bull Arena, Salzburg, Austria
FC Red Bull Salzburg v Wolfsberger AC

"I hope he puts me in the first team," Erling said to his team-mate and friend, Dominik Szoboszlai. Erling and the young Hungarian were both at a similar stage in their careers, and the two had quickly become friends.

The pair were always the last two on the training pitch, competing in shooting drills or trying out their latest ideas for new tricks. Skills were always more up

Dominik's street, but he wasn't anywhere near Erling's level when it came to shooting.

"The rumour is, Mu'nas is off to Sevilla," Dominik replied, referring to Salzburg's top scorer from the previous year, Mu'nas Dabbur. "So unless we're signing a big new striker, you've got no competition."

The only dealings in Salzburg's transfer window had been outgoings. First, manager Marco Rose had departed to join Borussia Mönchengladbach in the Bundesliga, and he'd been followed out of the door by Dabbur, Stefan Lainer, Hannes Wolf and Xaver Schlager, all to various clubs across Europe.

"It's like every time I check the news, we've lost another player," Erling said to Dominik in the training ground canteen one morning.

"It's a good thing, though!"

Erling was taken aback. "What do you mean?"

"It means we're going to get our chance in the first team. They think we're good enough!" Dominik said, leaning forward in his chair.

Talk of Erling's exploits at the U20 World Cup hadn't been confined to Norway. People from all over

Europe were now talking about the kid who'd scored nine goals in a single game.

Erling was now an international sensation.

It had given him a renewed sense of confidence on returning to Red Bull Salzburg. He felt sure he was in the right place, and he was happy to learn from the coaches and the players around him. So it hadn't bothered him that he'd made just two appearances in the previous season. But now he felt he was ready.

Nevertheless, he was still concerned that Salzburg might bring in a new striker. He'd been so confident that this was the right place for him, but now the manager in whom he'd placed his trust had departed. Erling began to wonder if it was too late to go back to Leeds.

But he needn't have worried. He started the first three games of the season, scoring four goals, including a hat-trick in the Austrian Cup. And to cap it all, it was clear that there was no new striker coming in. Erling was now Salzburg's main man.

Today was their fourth game of the season – and their first real test. Wolfsberger were a very good side, with the quality to compete at the top of the table. This was the first time that the new young Salzburg side were going to be put through their paces.

New manager Jesse Marsch took Erling aside before the start of the game.

"You're my man out there, Erling," he said, speaking with his typical American enthusiasm. "You're my lieutenant on the pitch. Lead by example, alright?"

Marsch paused for a moment, then added, "And I don't mean with goals and tricks and flicks. Your character is what sets you apart – your drive, your desire. So push their defenders, press them, harry them – and drag the team with you."

Erling nodded, feeling the familiar focus and confidence that had shaped his whole career.

Although Erling was one of the youngest players in his team, he felt like a leader. He had more first-team experience than any other player his age, so when Salzburg went 1-0 down inside ten minutes, it was Erling that the players looked to.

"There's 80 minutes left, boys!" he roared. "They'll crumble if we score one – and then we'll end up scoring five more! Don't change anything we're doing!"

Moments later, a chance arrived to get back on level terms. A cross by André Ramalho was flicked on by Patson Daka. Erling was in the right place at the far post to slam the ball home from close range.

"Come on!" Erling bellowed, waving his arms and getting his team-mates fired up. They were going to win this match and he knew it. Now they knew it too.

An own goal put Salzburg 2-1 up at half-time, but they knew that wouldn't be enough to secure the result. Marsch sent his team into the second half with high energy, searching for that third goal to kill the game.

They got their moment on a counter-attack, with Hwang Hee-chan dribbling and running at a defender. Erling was sprinting behind him, covering the ground at an electric pace. Hwang flicked the ball back into space, and there was nobody else who was going to get it.

"Erling's!" he screamed, taking the ball in his stride and drilling a left-footed finish past the keeper.

It was becoming Erling's signature finish now. Sprinting from his own end of the pitch to collect the ball, and then smashing it hard and low. It was difficult to stop – Erling knew that, once he got going, there was no defender in the world who could catch him.

Then Wolfsberger pulled a goal back to make it 3-2 and suddenly the pressure was on Salzburg to hold on. They'd taken their foot off the gas at 3-1, but now Erling was pressing hard on the pedal again.

He picked up the ball on the half-way line, bulldozed one defender to the floor and then skipped past the challenge of another. Then he displayed another of his attributes, spraying a brilliant pass to Hwang Hee-Chan.

And now it was time to run. He sprinted past the defenders, overlapping Hwang.

"Hwang! Now!" he bellowed once more.

The pass was simple and the finish even simpler. There was his hat-trick – his second of the season.

"You can never just score one or two, can you?" Dominik laughed, as they celebrated.

"I'll keep scoring until someone stops me," Erling chuckled.

So far, nobody could.

14

VIKING PRIDE

September 2019, Ullevaal Stadion, Oslo, Norway
Euro 2020 Qualifiers, Norway v Malta

"I told you! If you play for the U20s, good things will happen. Didn't I?"

"Yeah, I guess you did, Dad," Erling admitted.

"I remember my Norway debut. I was older than you are, but I hadn't even played in the Norwegian top division. People were really unsure – but then I made the World Cup squad!"

"I know, Dad," Erling replied.

He couldn't hear any more about the 1994 World Cup. It wasn't the only time that Norway had qualified for the World Cup, but the way his dad talked about it, it might as well have been.

Erling added four more Salzburg goals to his collection before the end of August, and by the end of the month he was sitting clear at the top of the goalscorers' charts.

But that wasn't the big news for him. The big news was tonight, in Oslo. Tonight he was making his debut for the Norway senior team.

It was his old U20 manager Pål Arne Johansen who had passed on the news that the Norway team manager, Lars Lagerbäck, wanted Erling in his 23-man squad for the Euro 2020 qualifiers, against Malta and Sweden.

It was an honour for Erling to play for his country, and the first person he told was his dad, the one person he knew who'd be more excited than he was.

"That's amazing, Erling!" Alf-Inge shouted down the phone with excitement. "Make sure you put everything into it, Erling," he added. "The feeling of playing for your country at a major tournament ...

I can't describe it. You have to make sure you experience that, Erling."

"I will, Dad," Erling promised.

It wasn't in his nature to give anything less than 100% anyway. He wouldn't even know how to take it easy. He'd proved that in the U20 World Cup when, after scoring eight goals and with his team 11-0 up, he'd still felt the need to push for more.

That was just how he was.

Lagerbäck named Erling in the starting line-up for Norway's game against Malta, alongside Josh King and Martin Ødegaard. On paper, Malta were an easier opponent than some of the other teams in Norway's qualifying group, teams such as Spain.

The manager pulled Erling to one side as the teams warmed up.

"Tonight is a brilliant opportunity for you to get on the scoresheet. Martin is a brilliant player and so are you. Make the right movements and he'll find you. You just have to finish."

As the players lined-up and Erling belted out the national anthem, along with the 28,000 Norwegians in the stadium, he suddenly realised why playing for his country was so special.

But it proved to be a frustrating Norway debut. The game was played at a much slower pace than Erling was used to at Salzburg, and he repeatedly found himself making runs that weren't being found by the midfielders.

He was taken off after 67 minutes and slumped into his seat on the bench, angry with himself for not scoring, angry with the team – and with his dad, for insisting that playing for your country was so amazing. It wasn't the hat-trick on his international debut he'd been dreaming of.

Norway won the game 2-0, but Erling still wasn't happy. Back in the changing room after the match, the manager spotted Erling's unhappiness and sat down next to him.

"You're angry, aren't you?" he asked, not waiting for a reply. "I get it. It takes a while to adjust to international football. It's probably much slower than you expected. But if it makes you feel better, I thought you played well. We all did."

"I didn't score," Erling replied.

"It's not always about scoring," Lagerbäck continued. "And trust me, son, you continue at the rate you're going, you're going to be scoring goals for Norway for years to come."

He paused for a moment, looking back out at the pitch.

"In fact, I think you'll break all our records."

15
NO TURNING BACK

October 2019, Anfield, Liverpool, England
Liverpool v FC Red Bull Salzburg

"I don't want to miss this one, but I don't think I can start," Erling confessed.

"That's very honest of you, Erling," Jesse Marsch replied. It seemed a genuine surprise to him. A player with Erling's drive and determination would normally do anything to play in a big game like this one, even if it was to the detriment of the team.

These kinds of players normally put themselves first.

But Erling was full of little surprises like this. Despite his desire to get goals, he was more than happy to let other players take the penalties. He would celebrate with the person who set him up, making sure that they got the recognition.

Marsch had seen this in Erling the very first time he'd met him. The Norwegian was a selfless leader, just as much as he was the selfish, prolific goalscorer.

"I'll tell you what, Erling," Marsch said. "Let's put you on the bench. Then maybe you can do the last half hour? Do you think you could do that?"

"I might miss the weekend's game," Erling replied.

"Don't worry about the weekend," Marsch chuckled. "We're talking about Anfield. You deserve the chance to play there."

Erling had returned to Salzburg with a spring in his step. He was now an international player at the tender age of 19, and, because Salzburg were champions of Austria, he was also playing in the Champions League. He had made it onto Europe's biggest stage – the competition he'd been dreaming of ever since he was a boy. But he wasn't just playing in Champions League games – he was scoring in them.

He followed up the international break with consecutive hat-tricks against TSV Hartberg in the Austrian Bundesliga and Genk in the Champions League.

But the big game was still to come. Since the draw, there was one game that everyone in Salzburg had been building up to. Liverpool.

The current champions of Europe – and probably the best team in the world right now – had been drawn in Salzburg's Champions League group.

Now, that was their next game – away to Liverpool at Anfield. And Erling was injured.

"I'm not missing this one," Erling had told Dominik as they'd warmed up on the training pitch. There was no way he wasn't going to play at Anfield against Liverpool.

But even as he'd said it, he felt himself straining. He could barely jog around the pitch, so there was no way he was going to be able to sprint past Virgil van Dijk. If he played, he'd just be a hindrance to the team.

And now, here he was, starting the game on the bench, just as Marsch had suggested.

Anfield was notorious all over Europe for being one of the most intimidating grounds for visiting players. The fans were loud and passionate, and when they got going you could barely hear yourself think.

Yet tonight, Erling found himself unimpressed by the noise. He didn't find it intimidating in the slightest. In fact, he could hear the Salzburg fans in the corner more than he could hear the Liverpool crowd.

Erling leaned towards Patrick Farkas, sitting next to him on the bench.

"I think we can win here," he murmured.

But he'd barely finished speaking when Liverpool scored. Anfield erupted and suddenly Erling realised what everybody meant about the stadium. He couldn't even hear Farkas' response to his comment over the noise of the crowd.

Liverpool were on top now, and they quickly added a second through Andy Robertson. It looked as if Salzburg were sinking without trace, just another of Liverpool's victims in their relentless pursuit of another title.

Mo Salah added a third, before Hwang Hee-chan pulled one back. At half-time Salzburg trailed 3-1.

"We need you up there, Erling," Dominik Szoboszlai told him in the dressing room. "There's space in behind them – you'd get goals, I'm sure of it."

"I'll be on soon," he replied. The injury that had plagued him for the last week had seemed to disappear since his arrival in Liverpool. All he wanted now was to get out on the pitch.

Ten minutes into the second half, Minamino pulled another goal back for Salzburg. Then, almost immediately, Marsch turned to Haaland and gestured for him to get ready.

"The game's there for the taking, Erling," he said. "They're on the back foot. This is the biggest stage – prove to everyone you belong here."

Erling had only been on the pitch a few minutes when he got his chance. Minamino skipped away into the box, drawing the attention of van Dijk. Erling waited at the back post, knowing that any ball across the box would be his.

Minamino's ball was perfect. Finding himself in acres

of space, a couple of yards out, Erling had no problem getting the goal – he wouldn't score an easier goal all season. It was now 3-3.

He sprinted in front of the Salzburg fans, waving his arms aloft in celebration.

"Let's win this now!" Marsch shouted across the pitch.

Then, 10 minutes later, Salah poked Liverpool back ahead. Salzburg had used all their energy to get the game back to 3-3. They were spent, and had nothing left.

On paper, a 4-3 defeat wasn't a terrible result, but it felt much, much worse. As Erling trudged off the pitch, he ran straight into Jürgen Klopp.

"You're a great player, kid," Klopp said, his face beaming. "Are you sure we can't have you at Liverpool?"

"Maybe one day," Erling replied, not quite in the mood to talk.

But as he stared out of the plane's window on the flight home, he thought about what Klopp had said to him. He couldn't avoid the truth any more. He was on the big stage now – and there was no turning back.

16
PACK YOUR BAGS

January 2020, Erling's House, Salzburg, Austria

"You know you've got a release clause, don't you?" Alf-Inge told his son.

Erling shrugged. "I guess so, but I don't pay much attention to all that stuff."

"Well, you do," Alfe-Inge continued. "It's about 20 million – so if any team wants you, they're going to have to pay that."

By the end of 2019, Erling had scored a massive 28 goals in just 22 games for Salzburg. He'd broken a number of Champions League records, including becoming the first teenager to score in their first five matches in the competition.

He'd always vaguely followed the transfer rumours in the press, and although he'd always tried to be humble, from what he'd seen, 20 million seemed pretty low, considering how people were talking about him.

"So, who's likely?" Erling asked his dad.

"Well, I mean … You don't *have* to go. You've not been at Salzburg that long – it might be good to stay a bit longer."

"You're just worried I might join Man United!" Erling laughed, knowing full well that, as an ex-City player, his dad would hate it if he joined their rivals.

"Well, so far only Borussia Dortmund have made a solid offer," Alf-Inge said, letting the thought hang in the air.

Erling hesitated.

Borussia Dortmund. They weren't on the same level as Man U or Juventus, but they were a massive club. Even better, they had a reputation for developing young players, especially strikers. Robert Lewandowski, Pierre-Emerick Aubameyang and Marco Reus had all developed into world-class players at Dortmund.

It was an easy decision.

Just days after the January transfer window opened, Erling's bags were packed for Germany.

17
THE MAN

February 2020, Signal Iduna Park, Dortmund, Germany
Champions League, Borussia Dortmund v PSG

"This is your competition, kid. We know it – *they* know it," Borussia Dortmund's manager, Lucien Favre, told Erling. "I don't want to give you too many instructions. Sancho, Hazard, Reyna and Witsel will all pick out your runs."

Erling had instantly adjusted to life in Germany, scoring seven goals in his first three Dortmund games, despite having a slight injury. Dortmund were nipping at the heels of Bayern Munich in the league, but tonight their attention turned to a different competition, one that Erling loved – the Champions League.

And their opponents were the French giants PSG.

This game was a different proposition to anything he'd experienced at Salzburg. When the Austrians had gone to Anfield, they'd been massive underdogs with nothing to lose. But here at Dortmund, there was a level of expectation. There was pressure on them to deliver the goods, even against a team like PSG.

Erling had thought that the atmosphere at Anfield was intimidating, but Dortmund was something else. The famous "yellow wall" was a sea of flags and banners, with a huge cacophony of noise echoing around the stadium. These were the nights the fans loved.

"I wouldn't want to be a PSG player," Jadon Sancho remarked.

"How are you doing, Erling?" Polish right-back Łukasz Piszczek asked, putting a hand on his shoulder. "This must be a big night for you."

"Yeah, I feel good. I just want to get out there."

Erling was being honest – he did feel good. The atmosphere gave him an extra burst of energy. These were the big occasions that he loved.

In fact, these were the moments that every footballer lived for. PSG were littered with superstars – Kylian Mbappé, Neymar, Ángel di María, Thiago Silva … This was a chance for Erling to get his name up alongside theirs and really announce himself to the rest of world football.

Dortmund started well, with chances falling to both Sancho and Erling, but the Norwegian could only shank his shot into the side netting.

At half-time, the score was still 0-0, but the atmosphere in the Dortmund dressing room was very positive.

"They can't match your pace," Erling remarked to Jadon. "You get in and I'll be right with you. If you find me, I will finish."

Twenty-five minutes into the second half, the moment came. Hakimi's cross was stabbed goalwards by Raphaël Guerreiro. The ball cannoned into Erling, but as the ball stayed in the air, he was able to turn in a flash, take the ball in his stride and scoop it into the net with his right foot.

He took one glance at the linesman, fearing a possible offside and VAR review, but he decided to celebrate anyway, sprinting away towards the Dortmund fans as they leapt into the air.

He sat cross-legged on the floor in a meditation pose – his now signature celebration.

"Yeah, boy!" Guerreiro roared in his face.

After a brief VAR check, the goal was given and Dortmund were 1-0 up. They were determined to add to their lead, but PSG had other ideas.

Mbappé fired in a cross to Neymar, who tapped it over the line, putting the Parisians on level terms. Now they had the wind in their sails.

Erling grunted and narrowed his eyes. All the talk in the press before the match had been about Haaland versus Mbappé, and he was desperate to make sure that he came out as the winner of that duel.

Barely a couple of minutes after PSG's equaliser, Erling got his moment. A driving run from Gio Reyna allowed him to play a pass into Erling's feet. He took one touch to take it into his stride and then lashed at it with his left foot.

To those watching, it may have looked like a wild shot, but Erling knew exactly what he was doing. It was perfectly placed, flying into the top corner, past the despairing dive of the keeper. There would be no VAR checks on this one. That was a definite goal.

As he was mobbed by his team-mates, Erling collapsed to the floor and stared up at the night sky. He soaked up the deafening noise of the crowd, all chanting "HAALAND!"

Dortmund managed to hold on for the win, giving them the advantage going into the second leg.

"Haaland v Mbappé, huh? That's the new Messi v Ronaldo, I reckon," Axel Witsel said to Erling.

"Well … " Erling said with a laugh, as he clapped the home crowd, not sure what to say about that comparison.

"Well, we sure know who won that battle tonight!" Guerreiro interrupted. "Haaland is the man!"

18
INTERNATIONAL UNDERDOGS

September 2020, Windsor Park, Belfast, Northern Ireland
Northern Ireland v Norway

"Just as we were really getting going," Jadon texted Erling. "It's not right, man. We were really challenging Bayern!"

Erling agreed. Dortmund had a young and vibrant team and he felt that they could have won the title this year, if they'd kept the team together and fully fit.

They had lost to PSG in the Champions League

second leg, and they were several points behind Bayern in the title race. It looked as if Erling was going to finish his first season in Germany trophyless.

But then their momentum had been stopped when the COVID-19 pandemic cut football's season short. When the season restarted, the team failed to recapture any of their previous form to challenge for the title.

The new season didn't start until the end of September, but before that came the international fixtures. Erling was yet to score for his country, but he was very keen to change that. Norway were putting together a good team and had a real opportunity to qualify for a major tournament.

After a defeat against Austria, Norway travelled to Belfast to take on Northern Ireland, a team who had qualified for the last European Championship. The game was a Nations League fixture, but finishing top of the group would put Norway in with a real shot of qualifying for the next Euros.

Erling would be joined up front by fellow Bundesliga striker, Alexander Sørloth.

"We've got two of the best strikers in Germany,

Alex," Erling said. "If they can feed us, we'll get goals."

"Don't get carried away," Sørloth reminded him. "Remember – the best teams are always built on defence."

"Let Ajer, Hovland and Thorsby focus on stopping Northern Ireland – and we'll do the business at the other end," Erling replied, naming some of Norway's key defensive players. He had a good feeling about tonight's game. Having won a number of trophies at club level in Austria, he was keen to translate that to the international stage.

"We can make a real announcement tonight, boys!" Lars Lagerbäck told the squad. "We can let the world know that Norway mean business once again!"

Within two minutes, Norway took the lead, with Mohamed Elyounoussi volleying in from Stefan Johansen's brilliant pass.

"I thought you two were the best strikers in Germany," Mohamed joked, "but it's me doing all the work!"

"Give us time!" Sørloth laughed.

"Well, I still think you should have squared it!" Erling grinned.

Northern Ireland poked themselves level just five

minutes later, and once more the pressure was on Norway.

But, a minute later, they were back in front. Sørloth headed down a long pass and the ball bounced towards Erling. He received it on the edge of the box and rotated his body to half-volley it first-time into the left-hand corner.

"Come on!" Erling shouted. In two games, he'd gone from having no Norway goals to scoring two.

Within 20 minutes, Norway had a third. This time, it was Sørloth who tapped in at the back post, after a brilliant cross. Norway weren't just winning, they were running away with the game.

Norway got their fourth in the opening seconds of the second half. Erling burst through, outpacing the Northern Ireland defence and controlling the ball with ease. Now one-on-one with the keeper, for a brief moment he thought about how to finish it. But then in the corner of his eye he spotted Sørloth's run – and he heard his strike partner shouting for the pass.

In a display of selflessness, he slipped the ball back to his team-mate, who tapped the ball into the open net.

"Cheers for that, Erling!" Sørloth said, as they celebrated together. "I assume you're going to want me to set you up now."

"Well, I can't do everything!" Erling chuckled.

Despite only scoring once so far, Erling was delighted. Norway were working well together as a team, and they were showing that they could compete with any team in Europe. They were here to be counted.

Ten minutes later, Erling got his second. A header from Elabdellaoui played him in. This time, there was no doubt in his mind. There was no chance he was going to square it. He opened up his body and whipped the ball hard into the top corner.

Norway were now 5-1 up – and Erling had two!

There weren't any fans in the stadium because of the coronavirus pandemic but, even if there had been, Erling imagined that the Northern Ireland fans would have been so stunned into silence by the scoreline that their presence wouldn't have made a difference.

At the full-time whistle, Lagerbäck caught up with Erling. "Keep playing like that, son, and the good results will keep on coming – for club and for country."

19
CLASH OF THE GOAL MACHINES

March 2021, Allianz Arena, Munich, Germany
Bayern Munich v Borussia Dortmund

"We've not started the season well, boys, but we can turn this around," the new manager, Edin Terzić, told them. "We can still qualify for the Champions League, and if we do well in the cups, we can finish this year with a trophy!"

It had been a disappointing season for Dortmund. The squad that the club had put together hadn't quite had the strong run of form that they'd hoped for. Injuries hadn't helped, and then there had been a change of management before the new year, with assistant Edin Terzic´ taking over from Favre.

Terzic´ was a breath of fresh air after the way that Favre had finished his time as Dortmund manager. He was closer with the players and was less concerned with tactics and getting results on the pitch. He was more focused on having fun and playing football the way they'd all done when they were younger.

"The results will follow," Terzic´ would always say. And the players believed him.

Erling himself had been in brilliant form. He'd struggled with injuries for large parts of the season, but when he'd been fit, he'd been scoring goals. Four against Hertha Berlin, two against Leipzig, and another two against Gladbach.

He'd maintained this in the Champions League, which was fast becoming his own personal competition, scoring six goals in the group stage.

"You're basically in a one-on-one battle with Lewandowski for the Golden Boot!" Jadon Sancho told him, after both players had scored in yet another weekend.

It did seem that way, although it seemed to Erling that, every time he scored, Robert Lewandowski would score three more. He was untouchable.

But the next match was the big one. The two players would be going head to head, Lewandowski v Haaland, in the clash of the giants – Bayern v Dortmund.

Bayern were running away with the title yet again, whilst Dortmund were languishing in sixth, still a few points away from Champions League qualification.

"This is a good time to get one over on Bayern, while they're least expecting it," Terzić told his players before the game. The stands were still empty because of the coronavirus pandemic, so although Dortmund were playing Bayern in Munich, there wouldn't be a hostile home crowd to make the job harder.

"I know you're keen to get one over Lewandowski aren't you?" Reus said to Erling, as they left the dressing room.

"I just want to win," Erling replied, keeping it short.

"You can't fool me, Erling," Reus replied. "I know

you're desperate to beat him, prove you're the best striker."

"Well, maybe we can do both," Erling grinned.

Dortmund got their first chance inside two minutes, when Axel Witsel's blocked shot was deflected towards Erling on the edge of the box. He took one touch to get the ball out of his feet, then weighed up his options. Thorgan Hazard was making a run to Erling's left, but the space ahead of the Belgian was crowded.

There was only one option. A shot.

He smacked it hard with his left foot and rifled an effort towards goal. It flicked off the bottom of Boateng's boot, flew up into the air and past the dive of Manuel Neuer.

Erling wheeled away in celebration, sliding along his knees in front of the empty stands.

"That's 1-0, Erling against Lewandowski!" Reus shouted to him as they celebrated.

"That's 1-0, Dortmund against Bayern!" Erling reminded him.

They were sending a message to the rest of Germany that Dortmund were still a force to be reckoned with.

A few minutes later, Dortmund came forward again. Guerreiro slipped a brilliant pass into Thorgan Hazard, with Erling chasing after them at full speed.

"Thorgan! Hit me!" Erling roared, his voice the loudest in the stadium.

The Belgian winger played the ball instantly and Erling was in the right spot to tap it into the back of the net.

"2-0!" Reus bellowed. "Come on!"

"Let's get some more now!" Erling shouted back to him.

But Bayern weren't going to take this lying down. The red onslaught began and Erling could only watch from the other end of the pitch as they peppered the Dortmund goal with shots.

After 25 minutes, Lewandowski got a goal back, and just before half-time he scored a penalty to level things up. It was now 2-2, with Erling and Lewandowski scoring all the goals.

"Everything I do, he just seems to match it," Erling muttered.

After an hour, Erling's night got worse as he was

forced to limp off with an injury. He had to watch from the sidelines as Bayern got a late winner to clinch the game.

And then, minutes later, Lewandowski sealed his hat-trick to make it four.

"This is the last time," Erling muttered to himself once more. "Next time, I'm going to beat him."

20
CUP FINAL

May 2021, Olympiastadion, Berlin, Germany
DFB-Pokal Final, RB Leipzig v Borussia Dortmund

"You've earned your right to be here, lads," Terzic´ said, leaning in close and looking at each of the players. "Reaching a final is a brilliant achievement, but it's not the full job, it's a job incomplete. We don't even have one hand on the trophy yet."

Erling sat in silence, thinking about his manager's words. For what felt like the first time all season, they had pretty much everyone fit. Erling, Jadon Sancho, Marco Reus, Mats Hummels, Jude Bellingham. It was their strongest squad.

"We know what Leipzig can do," Terzić continued. "They're a good side, but we're better. If we hit the ground running, we'll cause them problems and win this game!"

He raised his arms, trying to stir up the players. He needn't have bothered – every player in the room was ready for this one. Erling had already won trophies in Austria, but for many of his Dortmund team-mates this was their first opportunity to win a major trophy.

"You must know some of the Leipzig team from when you were at Salzburg, Erling," Marco Reus said, turning to him. "And Sørloth is Norwegian. Any tips?"

"Honestly, let's not worry about them," Erling replied. "We play our game and it doesn't matter what they do. They can't stop me and Jadon."

"Right answer," Reus said with a smile.

Erling hadn't been joking when he'd spoken to Reus. He knew that he and Jadon Sancho were in sensational form. If they got going, it would be very difficult to stop them. Dortmund had played second fiddle to both Leipzig and Bayern in the last few years. A big win tonight would once more send a message to the rest of Germany.

It would also add another trophy to his collection – and, unlike the trophies he'd won in Austria, this time he'd been a big part of the winning team.

A few moments later, they were out on the pitch, feeling the eerie atmosphere in the empty stadium. Erling hadn't quite got used to playing without crowds, and in a massive stadium like this it was even more evident.

"Let's get an early goal," Sancho said to Erling, reading his mind. "Make our own atmosphere!" The two of them had formed a prolific partnership in Dortmund's attack and they understood each other perfectly.

Within five minutes, Sancho got what he'd asked for. Erling slipped the ball back to Mahmoud Dahoud, who laid it off to Sancho. The winger took one touch, before cutting inside onto his right foot. He struck it hard and fast, rattling the ball into the far corner.

GOAL!

"Yes, Jadon!" Erling roared, chasing after his team-mate. It was a dream start to the final and Leipzig were shell-shocked. For 20 minutes they couldn't get the ball off Dortmund, but the yellow-and-blacks couldn't find the breakthrough to get a second goal.

"Get me the ball and I will score," Erling told his captain, Marco Reus. Following the advice that Ole Gunnar Solksjær had given him at Molde, Erling had studied Leipzig's centre-backs in the opening minutes of the game. He knew he had the beating of them – he just needed the opportunity to show it. He needed the ball.

Moments later, the chance came. Reus won the ball in midfield and instantly played it to Erling's feet. Erling sprinted towards the goal, pursued by the Leipzig centre-back, Upamecano.

Using his strength, Erling leant into him, easing him away and giving himself some space. With that space, he got the ball onto his left foot and side-footed it into the corner of the goal.

2-0!

Now Erling had his goal as well – a goal in a cup final too! It may have been his most important goal yet.

"You made Upamecano look tiny, Erling!" Sancho laughed, gesturing to the centre-back Erling had blasted out of his way.

"Nobody gets between me and a goal," Erling replied.

Just before half-time, Reus burst forward and laid the ball off to Sancho, who had an easy job of placing it past the keeper. Dortmund were now 3-0 up. They weren't just winning the cup – they were running away with it!

"I guess you'll want a hat-trick now," Erling said to Jadon at half-time.

"Don't worry, I still don't expect you to pass to me," he replied with a wink.

The second half was uneventful, until Dani Olmo fired a delicious strike home from long range to make it 3-1. Suddenly, Leipzig had their tails up and Dortmund were the team under pressure.

"Let's not lose this now!" Erling shouted. "Let's seal this with another goal!"

Erling had never been one to hold out for a win in a game of football. He always wanted to keep scoring goals.

But with Leipzig pushing for another goal, there was plenty of space for the Dortmund players to run into.

They soon won the ball back, played a long pass forwards and Jadon Sancho chased after the ball down the right wing. Dortmund had three against two inside the Leipzig half.

"Yes, Jadon!" Erling called.

Despite being on a hat-trick, Jadon played the ball to Erling on the edge of the box. The pass was a little behind the Norwegian and he had a yellow shirt to his left, but he still decided to shoot.

He pulled back his left foot and fired a shot towards goal, slipping as he did so. The ball looped up into the air and evaded the reach of the keeper, who could do nothing about the ball bouncing past him and into the goal.

"I guess you'll want a hat-trick as well now!" Jadon said, as they celebrated.

"Nah. I just want the trophy now."

Dortmund were now 4-1 up and cruising. A few minutes later, when the ref blew the final whistle, Erling collapsed onto the pitch. They'd done it!

With the medal around his neck, Erling could finally get his hands on his first Dortmund trophy.

"First of many," Erling said to Jadon, who replied with a smile.

Erling didn't know whether his future lay at Dortmund or elsewhere, but he knew this wouldn't be the last time he won a trophy. This wouldn't be the last time he came off the pitch having scored in a final.

He was just 20 years old and his career was still just beginning. He'd already achieved more than he could ever have imagined.

But he wasn't done yet. He wanted to be the best player in the world.

Where would that take him next?

21
CITY

October 2022, Etihad Stadium, Manchester, England
Man City v Man United

"It was always going to be City, wasn't it?" Erling's dad, Alf-Inge, said.

After another injury-hit and trophyless season, Erling had been forced to weigh up his options at Borussia Dortmund. Despite playing just 30 games, he'd scored 29 goals and had finished the season as one of the top scorers in Europe.

But Dortmund had been miles off the pace in the Bundesliga and had got nowhere near the Champions League or DFB Pokal trophies.

If Erling wanted to advance his career, if he wanted to start competing for big prizes again, the time had come to move on.

He'd had his pick of teams from across the world. Barcelona and Real Madrid had both expressed interest, as had Bayern Munich. And there were rumours that PSG, Manchester United, Liverpool, Chelsea and Juventus had all been putting in offers.

But, for all that, there was only one club that Erling had his heart and mind set on. Manchester City.

They had won the Premier League for the last two years, they were coached by Pep Guardiola, one of the best managers in the world, and – perhaps most importantly – they were the team with whom his dad had made his name.

On top of that, City were missing a striker following the departure of club legend Sergio Agüero, so the timing couldn't be better.

Even better for Erling, Pep had made it clear that the

team would now be built around him. He was the man that Pep thought could lead them to the Champions League title – a title that had eluded City for so long.

"It had to be City," Erling told his dad. "I'm just glad it's worked out."

"With you, Erling, I never doubted it."

Alf-Inge might have been confident that the move to City would work, but Erling hadn't always shared that belief.

The first game of the season had been the Community Shield, pitting Manchester City against their big rivals, Liverpool.

It had been Erling Haaland against Liverpool's expensive new striker Darwin Núñez – and Erling had lost. Liverpool had won 3-1, with Núñez scoring. To make matters worse, Erling had missed a sitter.

Immediately after the game, he was thrust into the spotlight. Was he a waste of money? It had cost a lot to bring him to the Premier League and City were putting a lot of faith in him. Was he going to let them down?

But a week later, in his first Premier League game, Erling silenced all the critics and doubters with a clinical brace against West Ham. He followed that with two consecutive hat-tricks, plus goals in the Champions League. By the start of October, he was on 14 goals from just 10 games.

The next game was the big one – Manchester United, at home.

"So, two consecutive home Premier League hat-tricks," Alf-Inge continued. "Get another one today and you'll be breaking all sorts of records."

"Let's just focus on winning the game, Dad," Erling replied.

Despite his prolific start to the season, City weren't top of the league. Arsenal had started their Premier League season in even better form, and they were currently sitting in first place.

Erling had not come to England to score a lot of goals and then finish the season without a trophy. He'd done that already. He wanted a title – a trophy. And that started with a win today.

United hadn't started the season particularly well, but this was still a local derby. City couldn't afford to sit off – they would have to start quickly.

And that was exactly what they did. Inside eight minutes, City took the lead, when Phil Foden fired past David de Gea. United then weathered the storm, and Erling was almost reduced to the role of bystander, with touches few and far between.

But shortly before half-time, his moment came.

Erling hadn't always been great in the air, but as the ball was floated in from the corner, he rose high above the United defence and powered a header towards goal. It was blocked on the line by the boot of a United defender, but Erling was already wheeling away in celebration. He knew it was in.

Moments later, the goal-line technology agreed with him. The goal was given. Erling had his first of the afternoon – his 15th of the season.

There were just 10 minutes to go before half-time, more than enough for Erling and his team-mates to add more goals.

Just three minutes after Erling's goal, a delicate Kevin De Bruyne cross was floated into the box. Erling stretched for it and stuck out a long left leg, connecting with the ball and directing it into the bottom corner.

Two goals in three minutes! He was now on course for the hat-trick he'd been joking about with his dad before the match.

A minute before half-time though, Erling turned provider, sliding a ball across the box for Phil Foden to smash home.

"Now we're both on hat-tricks, Erling," Phil said. "I might get there first, you know!"

"You wish," Erling laughed.

City might have been 4-0 up, but they still couldn't afford to switch off. Not long into the second half, Antony pulled a goal back for the away side.

It didn't signal a United comeback, though. Instead, City kicked it up another notch.

Despite Phil Foden's jibes, it was Erling who hit his hat-trick first. Sergio Gómez's cross was pulled back and Erling swept home with his left foot. There it was – his third hat-trick for City, his third Premier League hat-trick in just his eighth game, and his 17th goal of the season.

It didn't take long for Phil to join him with a hat-trick of his own. Once again, Erling was the provider. He slipped the ball into the path of Foden, who took one touch and then blasted it into the top corner.

United managed to get two late goals, but the damage had already been done. City had thrashed them 6-3.

At full time, Erling handed Phil Foden the match ball. "You take it, Phil," he laughed. "I've already got about a hundred of them."

Erling walked around the pitch, applauding the fans and soaking up the atmosphere. He had never expected his Manchester City career to start as well as this.

He was now the leading striker in the Premier League. It was still early in the season, but he was already the favourite for the Golden Boot.

Yet Erling wanted more than that. He wanted titles, records. Now he was going to make it happen.

22
CHAMPIONS

June 2023, Atatürk Olympic Stadium, Istanbul, Turkey
UEFA Champions League Final, Man City v Inter Milan

"Today you have a chance to make history, guys," Pep announced, capturing the attention of the City players and silencing the chatter in the dressing room. "Inter know they are the underdogs, they will make it difficult for us to play. We are going to have to be on top form to beat them."

The City players were sitting in the dressing room

at the Atatürk Olympic Stadium, going through their final preparations before stepping out onto the turf for the Champions League Final. They all knew how momentous this game was – for Pep, for themselves and for the club.

"We cannot be complacent," Pep continued. "We were complacent against Chelsea in the final, two years ago, and we lost. Today we have to make sure we are switched on, from the first whistle to the last, guys."

As Pep turned to talk to each player in turn, Erling laced up his boots and reflected on the season so far.

For him, it had been a whirlwind first campaign in English football. He had broken almost every record there was to break, and he'd won trophies and awards that, before joining City, he could only have dreamt of.

It had been the best debut season for a Premier League player *ever*. He knew he was more than ready for today's game.

Last month, City had won the Premier League title, with Erling finishing – as predicted – as the season's top scorer and winner of the Golden Boot.

Then, just a week ago, City had beaten local rivals

Man United in the FA Cup Final to win Erling's second trophy. And all in his first season at the club.

But Erling wanted more.

If City could win today, they would claim an historic continental treble by adding the Champions League trophy to the season's haul. This was a trophy that City had never won, so a victory today would be even sweeter.

The club had battled hard to reach the final. After finishing top in their group, they'd been drawn in their round of 16 tie against RB Leipzig – a club familiar to Erling from his time in the Bundesliga.

Erling had scored an incredible five goals in the second leg of that tie, with City obliterating the German team 8-1 on aggregate.

In the quarter-final, City had faced German champions Bayern Munich – another team Erling knew well from his time at Borussia Dortmund.

City were on another level though, and Bayern hadn't even been able to get close. Erling had scored twice – plus an assist – as City had sailed through to the semi-final, winning 4-1 on aggregate.

Then, in the semi-final, City had faced Real Madrid,

the most successful club in Champions League history. City and Real were the two strongest sides left in the tournament, and many pundits had declared that whoever won that semi-final would likely go on to win the final.

After a tense 1-1 draw in the first leg, away at the Santiago Bernabéu, City had demonstrated their class with a 4-0 second-leg victory at home, securing their place in the final.

Just then, Erling's thoughts were interrupted by Pep, who had finished speaking to Kevin De Bruyne, to Erling's right.

Now Pep fixed his attention on Erling.

"You already know what your job is today, Erling," Pep began. "I want you to stick to the last defender and never leave him alone. Nobody has been able to handle you this season, and the Inter defenders won't be able to either."

"I won't give them a second's rest." Erling smiled confidently.

"If you can get yourself into the box, I'll cross it to you every chance I get," Kevin chimed in.

Theirs had been a prolific partnership throughout

the season, and Erling knew that if they could keep that up today, they would see goals.

As the teams trooped down the tunnel and out onto the pitch, Erling was met by the deafening roar of both sets of fans in the stadium, mixed in with the dying notes of the Champions League anthem.

Whatever the result today, Erling knew that this would be a day to remember.

City were on the front foot right from the kick-off. As expected, Inter's defenders were closely marking Erling and he was struggling to find space or create chances. But with Inter focusing mainly on him, that created more space for his team-mates.

Both Jack Grealish to his left and Bernardo Silva to his right were able to drive up on the wings, spreading the play and forcing the Inter defenders into a lot of running. Erling knew that this would cause them problems later in the game, when fatigue would set in.

Then, in the 36th minute, disaster struck. After a short sprint, Kevin De Bruyne pulled up sharply, holding his leg. Erling rushed over to him, but he knew it wasn't good news.

"My hamstring," Kevin began. "Looks like you're going to have to win this one without me, Erling," he added, grimacing.

Kevin couldn't continue and he was replaced by Phil Foden. City struggled to keep up the same level of pressure after the substitution, and soon it was half-time – with the score still 0-0.

The second half began in much the same way, with City struggling to find a way through the resilient Inter defensive wall.

Then, in the 68th minute, they finally broke through.

Manuel Akanji, Erling's former Dortmund team-mate, played a pass which split the Inter lines. Bernardo Silva's run was perfectly timed and he strode onto the ball before cutting it back into the box, towards Erling.

The Inter defenders scrambled to prevent Erling reaching the ball, but it didn't matter. He'd been the perfect decoy for Rodri, who steamed onto the ball and smashed it low into the bottom-right corner of the goal, far beyond the desperate reach of Inter keeper, André Onana.

GOAL!

The City players wheeled away in celebration, mobbing Rodri as the cheers of the City fans resounded around the stadium.

"I thought I was supposed to be this team's goalscorer," Erling laughed, embracing Rodri.

"You can be this team's defender now – we've got a lead to protect," Rodri grinned.

Inter had been shattered by the City goal and, after the referee got the game back underway, they struggled to mount any meaningful attack.

There were a couple of half-chances which the Inter forwards couldn't capitalise on, but there were no more goals.

As the final whistle blew, the City players and fans celebrated an historic win – their first Champions League trophy and their first continental treble.

For Erling, he'd won all this in his very first season at City. He was already a legend at the club.

For most players, winning the Champions League was the ultimate achievement, but for Erling it was only the beginning.

He wanted it all. This was just a step on the way.

As he joined his team-mates celebrating in the centre circle, he was already thinking about the next trophy he would win.

Looking back, Erling had never really expected to be here.

The boy from Bryne, Molde, Salzburg … He hadn't come through a fancy academy. He hadn't been coached by the very best. He'd had to work to get here. And now he'd made it.

And, at just 22, with his whole career ahead of him, he knew that he was just getting started.

HOW MANY
HAVE YOU READ?

Printed in the USA
CPSIA information can be obtained
at www.ICGtesting.com
JSHW021128051223
53240JS00004B/1

9 781948 585798